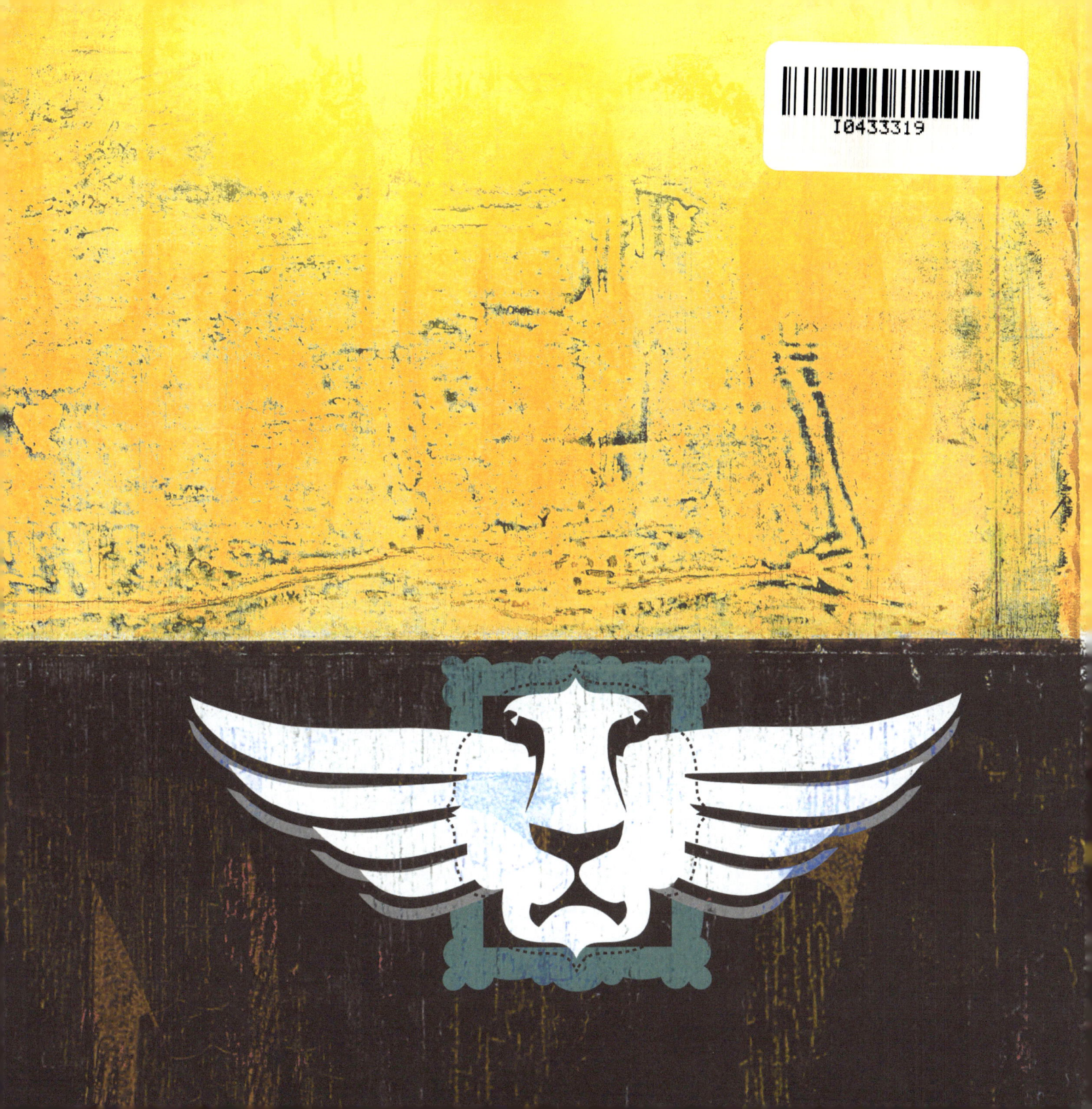

ART courage

The Art Courage Program

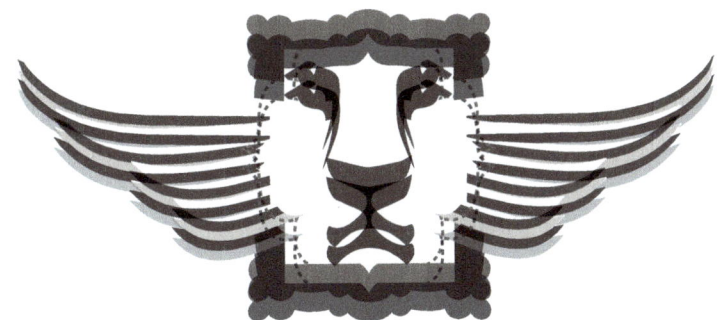

a therapeutic plan to free you from your fear of art

Katharine Whitcomb and **Brian Goeltzenleuchter**
Emotional Language Therapist Founder of *Contraposto Living*

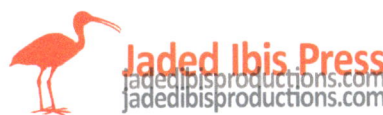

Jaded Ibis Press
sustainable literature by digital means™
an imprint of Jaded Ibis Productions

COPYRIGHTED MATERIAL

© 2014 copyright by Katharine Whitcomb and Brian Goeltzenleuchter

First edition. All rights reserved.

ISBN: 978-1-937543-63-1

Printed in the United States of America. No part of this book may be used or reproduced in any manner whatsoever without written permission from the publisher, except in the case of brief quotations embodied in critical articles and reviews. For information, email: questions@jadedibisproductions.com

Published by Jaded Ibis Press, sustainable literature by digital means™ An imprint of Jaded Ibis Productions, LLC, Seattle, WA USA

Book Cover Design & Creative Direction: Charmaine Banach
Layout & Design: Kristin Holda
Illustration: Brian Goeltzenleuchter

This book is available in multiple editions. For more information, please visit jadedibisproductions.com

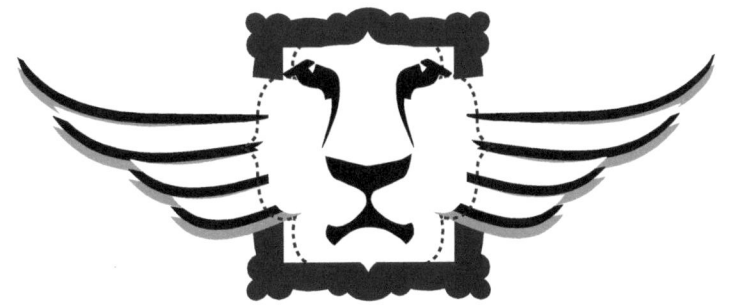

Non sum qualis eram*

I am not what I was

CONTENTS
The Art Courage Program

Introduction

Chapter One: The Art Courage Program Personal Audit for Self-Liberation
- Unit One
- Unit Two
- Unit Three
- Unit Four
- Unit Five
- Unit Six
- Unit Seven

Chapter Two: My Art Affirmation

Chapter Three: Intimacy With Art

Chapter Four: Simple Meditations

Chapter Five: Emergency Coping Techniques

Chapter Six: 3-Point Plan for Alleviating Art Anxiety

Chapter Seven: The Art Courage Program's Dear Person Letter

Chapter Eight: The Art Courage Program's Write Your Own Art Prescription

Conclusion

Author Biographies

Related Products from c (pronounced /k/)

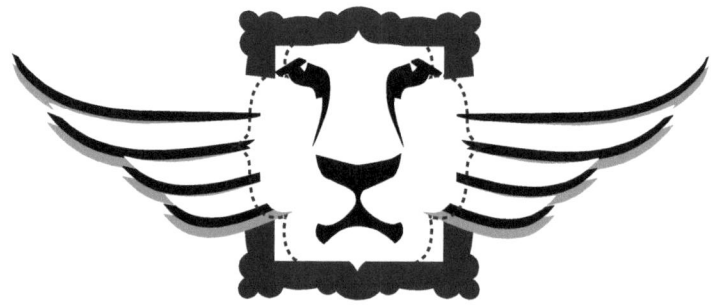

INTRODUCTION

We all want to heighten our levels of awareness and enrich our lives.

Encounters with art are one way to raise our perception and fulfillment. Occasionally, we run into internal roadblocks that hamper this process.

A negative reaction or interaction with art can be a sign that our lives are out of balance.

The Art Courage Program will provide you with a detailed plan to face the challenges and rewards of a new relationship with art.

I'll be your guide.

I'll show those of you who've been suffering with art anxiety how to move, step by step, through and beyond its darkness.

And I'll walk with all of you who are simply nervous, uneasy, confused or bored with art, and help you to discover new ways to help and heal yourself.

In *The Art Courage Program*, I'll give you the tools you need to successfully navigate your way to fulfillment with art.

I am confident that you can move beyond negative art reaction or art anxiety, learn from and be healed by your experiences, and find acceptance and even appreciation of art.

As an award-winning emotional language therapist and an art maker, I continue to be impressed by the strength and courage, as well as the vulnerability, of nervous and angry people.

I respect each person as a full partner in our healing work and I think of them as fellow travelers on the journey away from fear.

Partnering with c (pronounced /k/), the boutique healing wing of *Contraposto Living*, I have developed techniques that actively engage deeply anxious and fearful people. If you think you are one of those people, you are in good hands.

The Art Courage Program will equip you with the perspectives and attitudes, the mental, emotional, and physical techniques that you need to sustain yourself as you make your way through and beyond art anxiety.

This program is produced by c (pronounced /k/) as one of its sensory modalities, which also include the *Sonic Impact Series*, *Wellness Fragrances*, *Light Therapy* and *Adaptive Equipment*.

In this program you will receive:

- An easy-to-take Personal Audit for Self-Liberation to help you gauge the severity of your negative art reaction

- My Art Affirmation for reassurance in times of need.

- Simple, effective meditations that can enhance the chemistry of your brain and body, and make it easier for you to deal with and transform the beliefs and fears about art that have overwhelmed you.

- Institutionally-tested exercises with olfactory therapy, imaging, action/release, and breath unit techniques that can help you mobilize your body away from negative art reactions.

- The 3-Point Plan for alleviating intense instances of art anxiety.

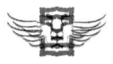 A helpful script of a Dear Person letter to ease your interactions in uncomfortable situations.

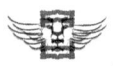 A guide for writing your own Art Prescription.

I have used *The Art Courage Program* for private instruction and in public workshops with great success.

Now, for the first time, I'm offering *The Art Courage Program*, to you, in a form you can use on your own at home.

As you work with *The Art Courage Program*, I'll be by your side, explaining and guiding you through various therapeutic processes, and leading you in exercises and experiments that you can use to explore and resolve the difficulties with art that trouble you.

At the end of the program, I'll give you examples of simple, practical Art Prescriptions for self-care; methods you can use every day to transform yourself mentally, physically and emotionally; methods that will help you move beyond your art anxiety.

This program challenges the typical approaches to discomfort with art that are prevalent in our society.

It has become all too common that symptoms of art anxiety are expressed publically through feigned condescension or apathy toward art, while privately the sufferer feels shame and inadequacy.

What I'm sharing with you is a comprehensive and effective model for healing the art anxiety that affects so many of us.

You can start to use *The Art Courage Program* right now to meet your unique needs and give you positive results that you will begin to experience immediately.

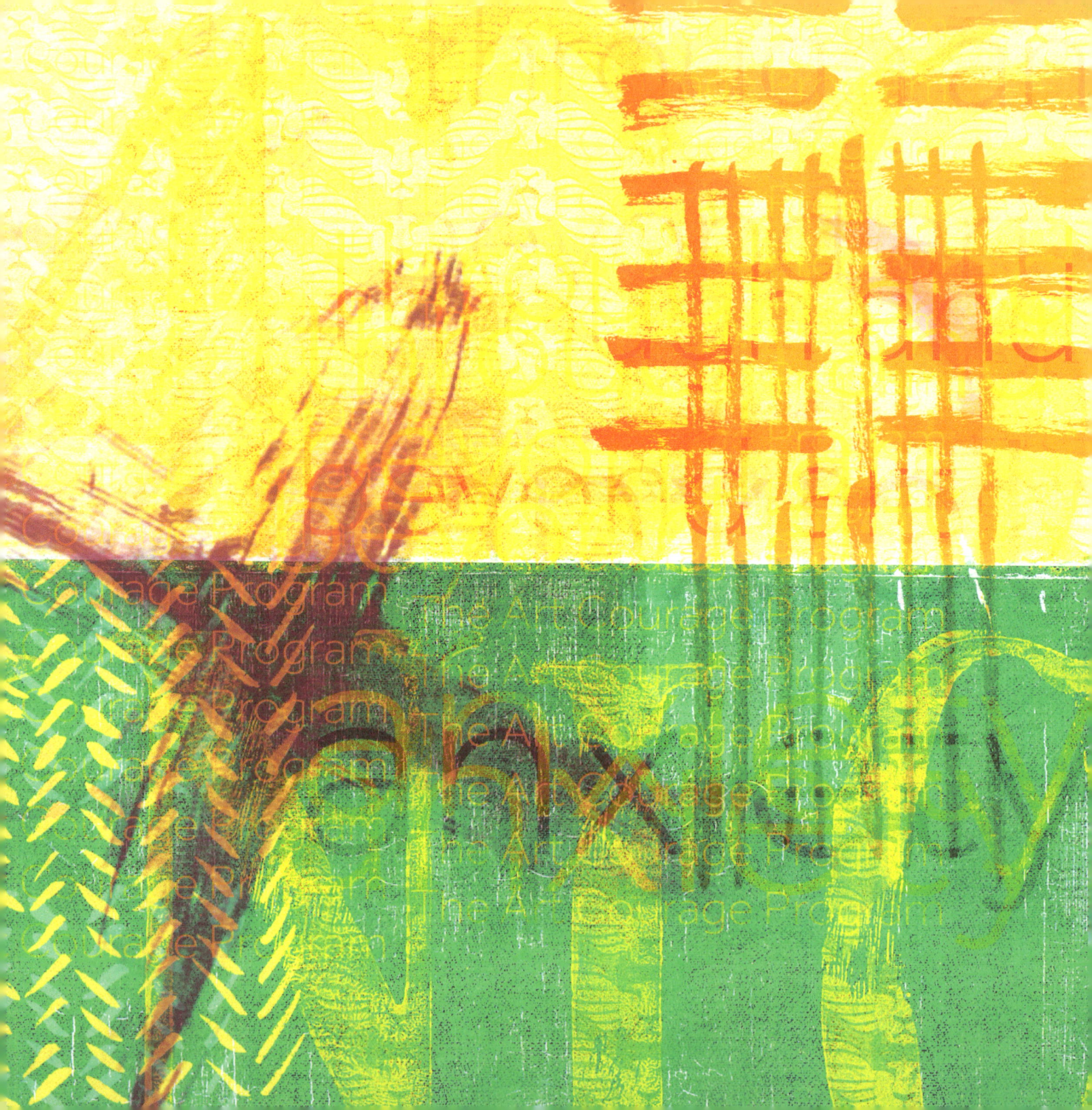

CHAPTER 1

The Art Courage Program
Personal Audit for Self-Liberation

A good place to begin to move away from art anxiety is to "audit" your fears and symptoms.

This will help with your self-examination process, and allow you to target your most troublesome reactions.

Let's begin—you will want to record your answers on a piece of paper as we go.

Keep track of how many "Yes" answers you have in each section of questions.

UNIT ONE

Do you experience sudden episodes of intense or overwhelming fear when you are exposed to art?

○ YES ○ NO

During these episodes, do you experience symptoms similar to the following: racing heart, chest pain, difficulty breathing, choking sensation, lightheadedness, tingling or numbness?

○ YES ○ NO

During these episodes do you worry about something terrible happening to you, such as embarrassing yourself, looking stupid, having a heart attack or dying?

○ YES ○ NO

Do you worry about having additional episodes?

○ YES ○ NO

UNIT TWO

Do you worry about a number of events or activities (such as a gathering near public sculpture, a gallery crawl or a party at an art-lover's house)?

○ YES   ○ NO

Is it difficult to control the worry?

○ YES   ○ NO

When you think of these events do you also have two or more of the following symptoms:

feeling "on edge"   ○ YES   ○ NO

feeling irritable   ○ YES   ○ NO

feeling out of control   ○ YES   ○ NO

muscle tension   ○ YES   ○ NO

sudden nausea   ○ YES   ○ NO

UNIT THREE

Have you experienced or witnessed a frightening or traumatic art reaction, either recently or in the past?

○ YES   ○ NO

Do you continue to have distressing recollections or dreams of the event?

○ YES   ○ NO

Do you become anxious when you face anything that reminds you of that traumatic event?

○ YES   ○ NO

Do you try to avoid these reminders?

○ YES   ○ NO

UNIT FOUR

Do you have recurring thoughts about art that feel intrusive and make you anxious?

○ YES ○ NO

On occasion, do you know that these thoughts are unreasonable or excessive?

○ YES ○ NO

Do you want these thoughts or images to stop, but can't seem to control them?

○ YES ○ NO

Do you engage in any behaviors (like rude outbursts, ridiculing others, making disparaging remarks, talking on your cellphone) or mental acts (like praying, singing silently to yourself, counting) in order to end these intrusive thoughts or images?

○ YES ○ NO

UNIT FIVE

Are you afraid of one or more of these basic social situations:

Taking a test with art on it?

○ YES ○ NO

Talking about art?

○ YES ○ NO

Eating near art?

○ YES ○ NO

Taking someone on a date and encountering art?

○ YES ○ NO

Do you get anxious or worried if you try to participate in these situations involving art?

○ YES ○ NO

Do you avoid these situations when possible?

○ YES ○ NO

UNIT SIX

Are you afraid of one specific object or situation, such as being given a piece of art, being taken to an art film, being asked your opinion of a painting, having to attend a poetry reading or getting a tattoo?

○ YES ○ NO

Do you get anxious or worried if you participate in those situations involving art?

○ YES ○ NO

Do you avoid these situations when possible?

○ YES ○ NO

UNIT SEVEN

Are you afraid of making a drawing?

○ YES ○ NO

Do you get anxious or worried if you draw?

○ YES ○ NO

Do you avoid drawing when possible?

○ YES ○ NO

Now add up how many "Yes" answers you made while taking the Personal Audit.

The range will be from:

0 — with zero equating you with someone comfortable viewing Andres Serrano's *Piss Christ*
to
27 — with you feeling uncomfortable in the presence of the most banal Thomas Kinkade print.

You can use your number as a guide number as you work out your Art Prescription later in this book.

You can gauge your level of discomfort and form a plan of therapeutic techniques to dispel this discomfort.

Personal Audit Scale

0-Andres Serrano's *Piss Christ*
1-Kasimir Malevich's *Suprematist Composition: White On White*
2-Gerhard Richter colour chart paintings
3-Marcel Duchamp's *Étant donnés*
4-Kurt Schwitters' collages
5-Robert Barry's *Inert Gas Series*
6-Piet Mondrian's *Composition II in Red, Blue, and Yellow*
7-Alberto Giacometti's *Walking Man*
8-Guerrilla Girls
9-Pablo Picasso's Cubist works
10-Frida Kahlo's *Henry Ford Hospital*
11-Michelangelo Merisi da Caravaggio's *Judith Beheading Holofernes*
12-Nicolas Poussin's *The Abduction of the Sabine Women*
13-Robert Rauschenberg's *Monogram*
14-Damien Hirst's *Cock and Bull*
15-Rosa Bonheur's *Ploughing in the Nivernais Region*
16-Pierre-Auguste Renoir's painting of women
17-Jean-Auguste-Dominique Ingres's *Grande Odalisque*
18-Gerhard Richter's *Abstract Paintings*
19-Rene Magritte's *La Condition Humaine*
20-Gerhard Richter's cycle *October 18, 1977*
21-Georgia O'Keefe abstracted flower painting
22-Henry Moore or Isamu Noguchi's sculptures
23-David Hockney's photographic collages
24-Leroy Neiman's mustache
25-Grant Wood's *American Gothic*
26-Komar & Melamid's *Most Wanted Paintings*
27-Thomas Kinkade's *A Quiet Evening*

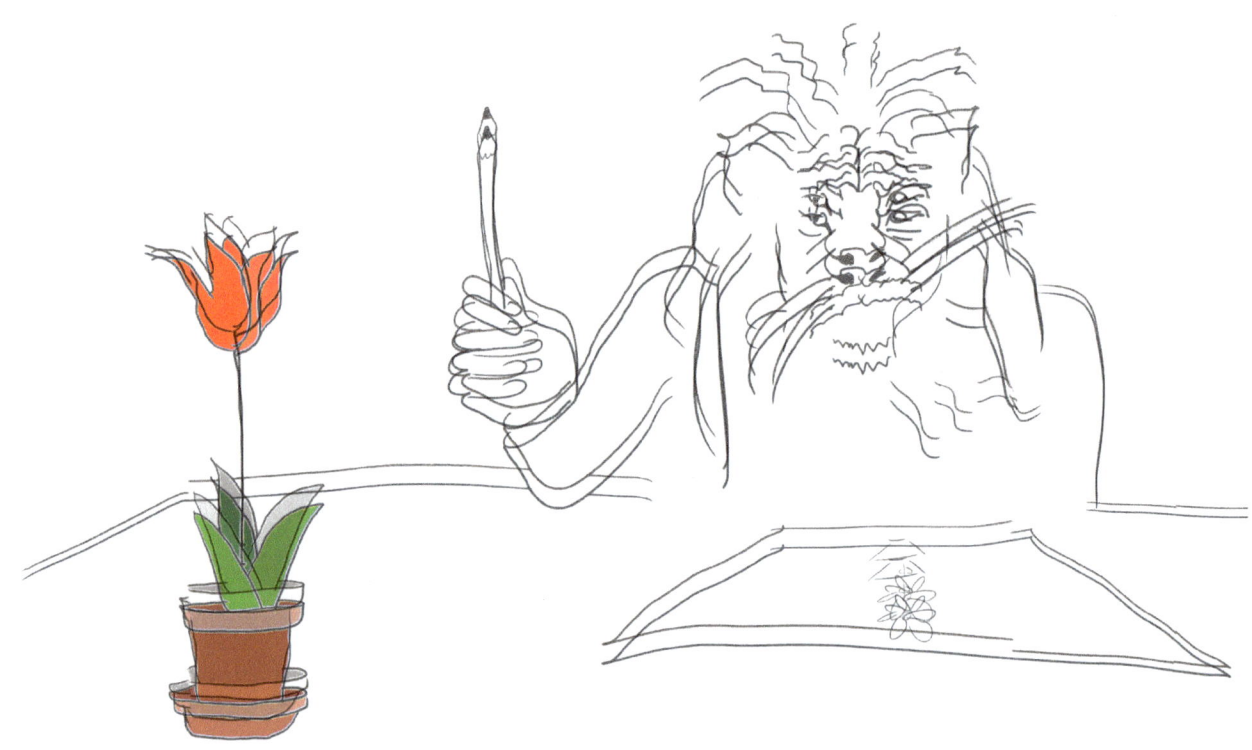

Do you get anxious when you draw?
Do you get anxious when you draw?

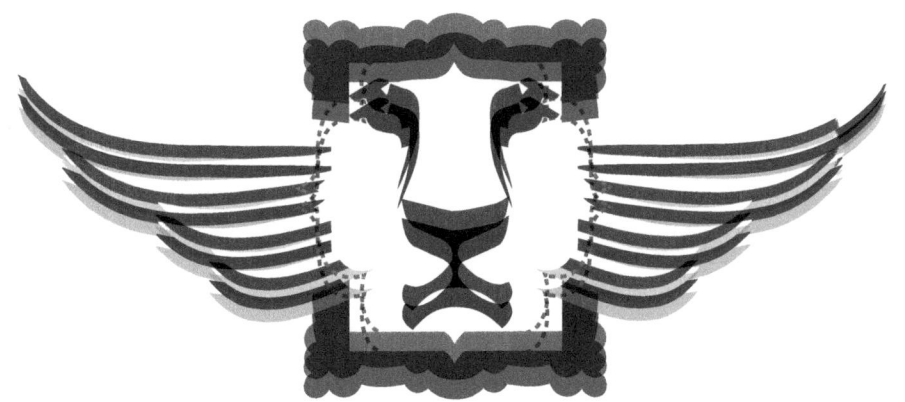

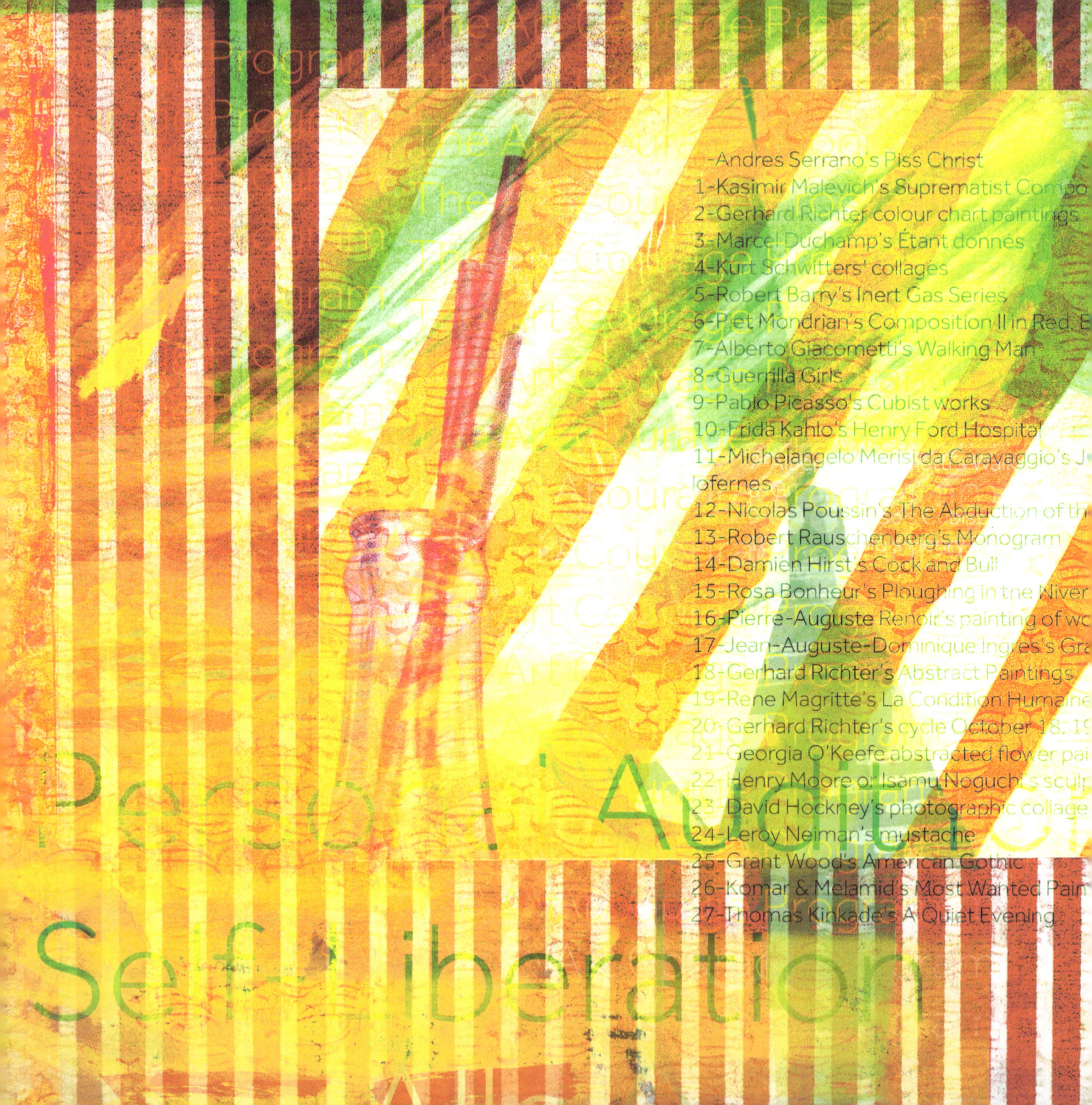

-Andres Serrano's Piss Christ
1-Kasimir Malevich's Suprematist Compo
2-Gerhard Richter colour chart paintings
3-Marcel Duchamp's Étant donnés
4-Kurt Schwitters' collages
5-Robert Barry's Inert Gas Series
6-Piet Mondrian's Composition II in Red, B
7-Alberto Giacometti's Walking Man
8-Guerrilla Girls
9-Pablo Picasso's Cubist works
10-Frida Kahlo's Henry Ford Hospital
11-Michelangelo Merisi da Caravaggio's J
lofernes
12-Nicolas Poussin's The Abduction of th
13-Robert Rauschenberg's Monogram
14-Damien Hirst's Cock and Bull
15-Rosa Bonheur's Ploughing in the Niver
16-Pierre-Auguste Renoir's painting of wo
17-Jean-Auguste-Dominique Ingres's Gra
18-Gerhard Richter's Abstract Paintings
19-Rene Magritte's La Condition Humaine
20-Gerhard Richter's cycle October 18, 19
21-Georgia O'Keefe abstracted flower pal
22-Henry Moore or Isamu Noguchi's sculp
23-David Hockney's photographic collage
24-Leroy Neiman's mustache
25-Grant Wood's American Gothic
26-Komar & Melamid's Most Wanted Pain
27-Thomas Kinkade's A Quiet Evening

CHAPTER 2
My Art Affirmation

Were you surprised that your number from the Personal Audit was high?

Does your art anxiety interfere with your everyday pleasure and enjoyment of life?

Take a moment right now to calm yourself.

Let's begin with My Art Affirmation.

This is a positive statement you can return to again and again in this program to reassure yourself.

Take a deep breath and exhale all the air completely out of your lungs.

Make yourself breathe deeply and quietly and let My Art Affirmation soothe you:

You are frightened and you feel yourself unbalanced.

You dread an art gallery and doubt your capacity to face it. Calm yourself.

This is the art we must deal with, and for today you will have strength. Rely on yourself.

Allow my coping strategies to ease your fears.

Permit them to bring you balance.

You do not have to face the art alone.

When you are frightened, it is because you are not grounded.

When you dread the unfamiliar, it is because you forget you have the tools within yourself to face the art.

You are not alone.

You are part of the public and you are surrounded by others.

When you remember your body and the bodies around you, what art can harm you?

Reach down and touch the floor.

You are here in the room in your body right now.

There is no harm when you rely on the world.

We have the means to successfully work through all your art fears.

Bring us the knotted up skein of your fear and we will untangle it.

To manage your fear is a thing of beauty.

A new relationship to art can be woven into your future.

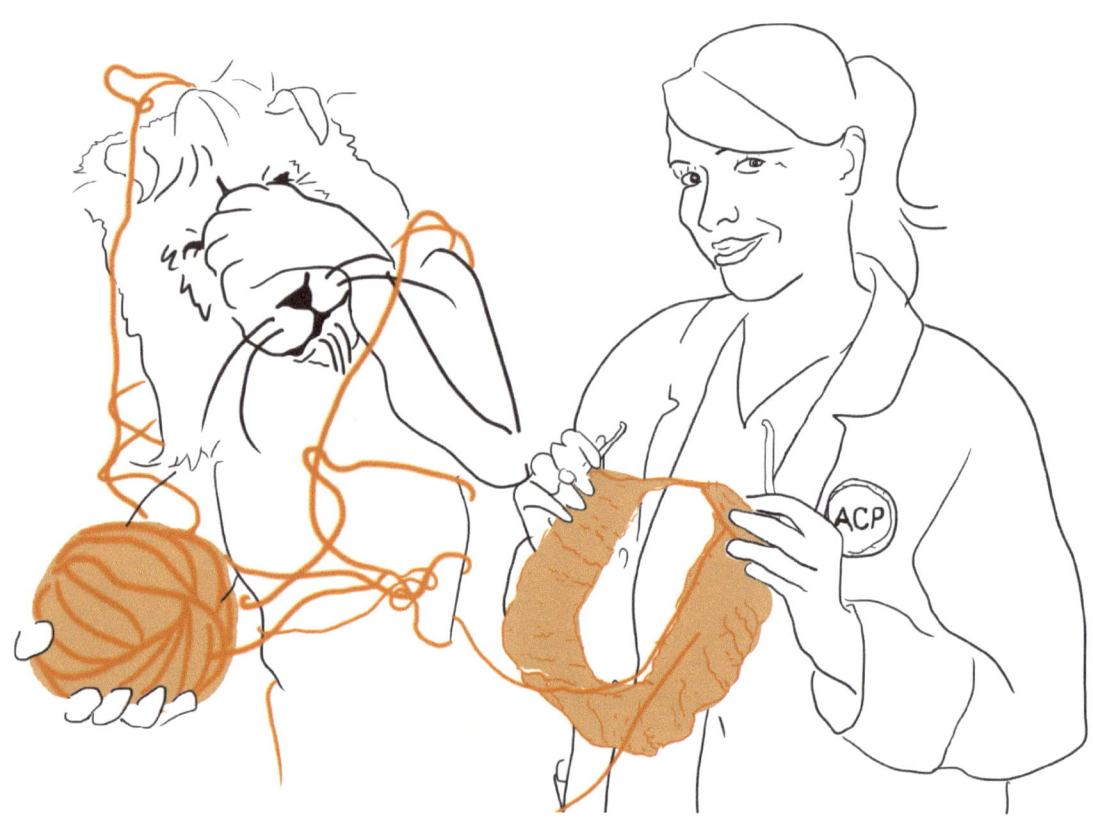

Bring us the knotted up skein of your fear and we will untangle it.

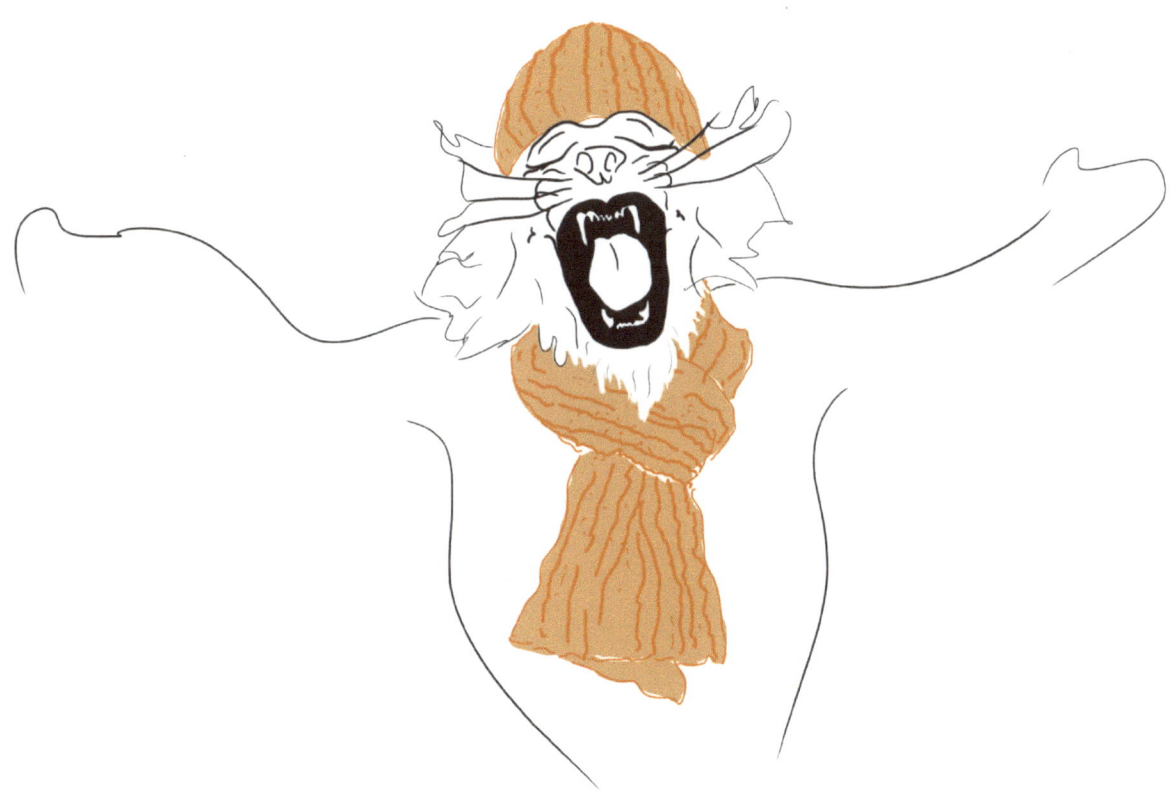

A new relationship to art can be woven into your future.

CHAPTER 3
Intimacy with Art

Fear is a natural reaction to moving closer to art.

It helps sometimes to try to understand our natural reactions as human beings towards things we fear.

Opening ourselves to art is like getting into an airplane and flying to a place we have never been. Despite our willingness to walk into the plane and take our seat, we may experience some fear.

Fear is a natural reaction to moving closer to art. And no one ever tells us to stop running away from art. We don't even need that kind of encouragement, but dissociating from fear is what we do naturally.

We habitually spin off and freak out when there's the merest hint of fear. We feel it coming and we check out.

It's good to know we do that—not as a way to beat ourselves up, but as a way to develop the best coping strategies.

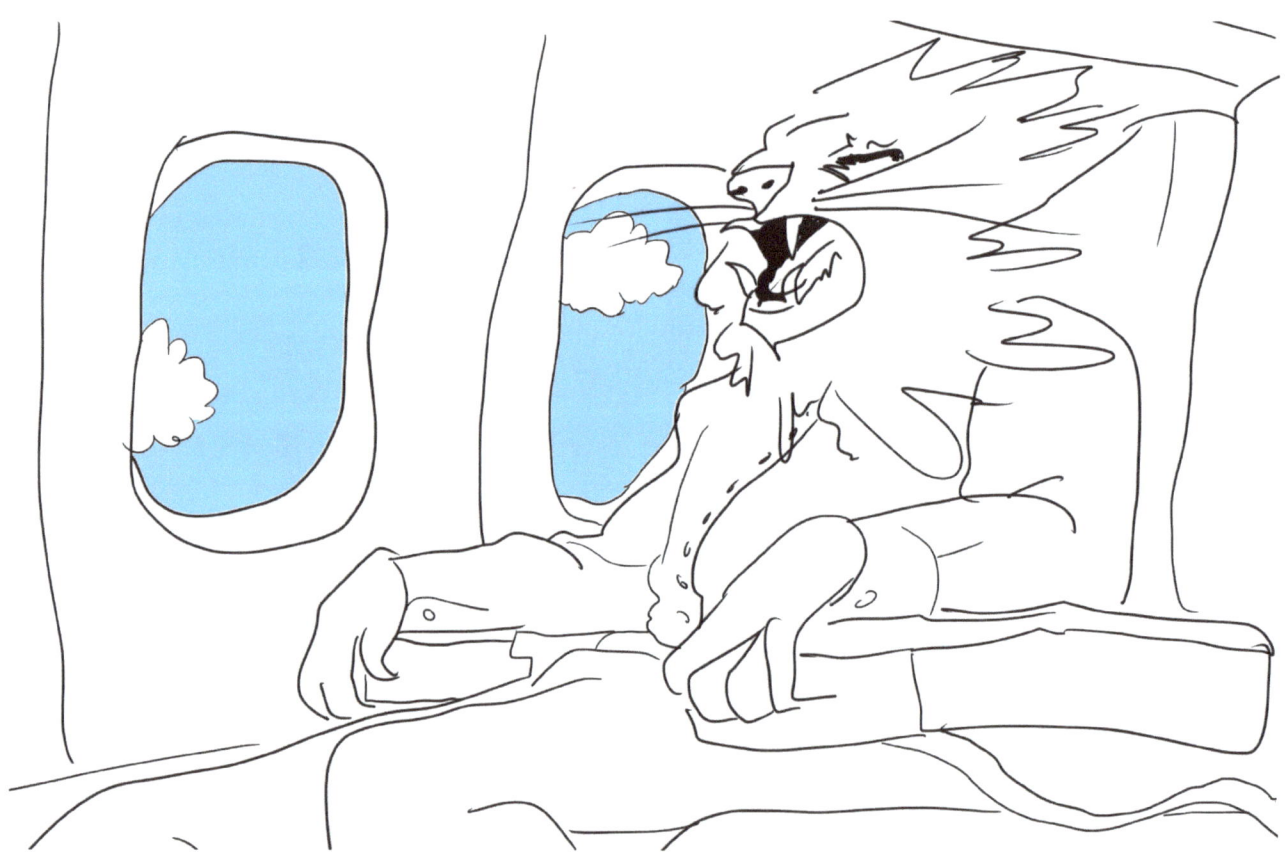

Keep your seat and stay on the plane!

The most heartbreaking thing of all is how we cheat ourselves out of the art in front of us.

This fear links us to a whole historical progression.

In the case of abstract art (like the Suprematist paintings of Kazimir Malevich) or conceptual art (like the instructions for art of Douglas Huebler), the space we observe contains objects that look easy.

They are easy, in a way, but they are frightening too, because of what they are missing.

We are so used to relating experience to our bodies.

We like to put ourselves into the painting or the sculpture. We like to think about how difficult it would be for us to create that piece of art.

We can relate to a physical setting.

We have been in a room looking at representational pictures many times before in our lives, but a gallery with no paintings may make us afraid.

A wall of color or a minimalist object may make us think we are stupid and missing something.

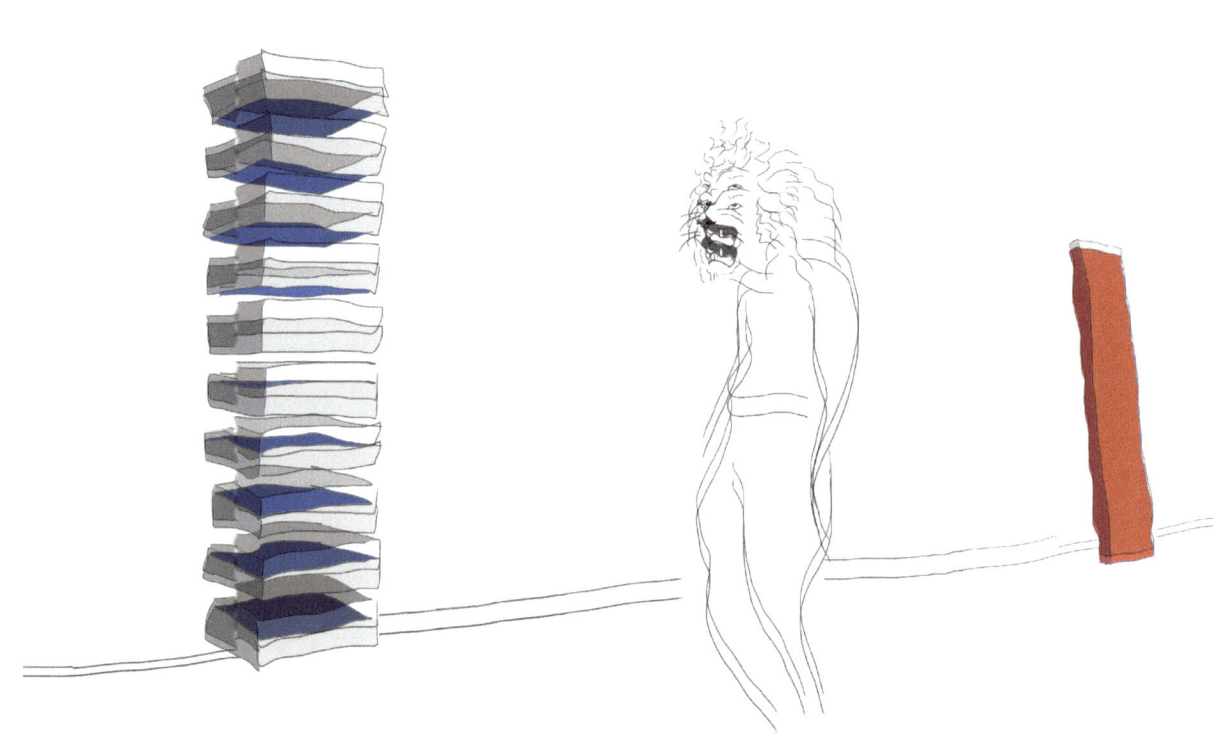

Art is not what we thought!
Art is not what we thought!

We may not know what to think about watching a film or smelling a scent instead of looking at a portrait.

So the next time you encounter fear of art, consider yourself lucky.

This is where courage comes in.

The trick is to keep your seat and stay on the plane, even when we find out that art is not what we thought! That's what we're going to discover again and again and again. Nothing is what we thought. I can say this with great confidence.

Art is not what we thought.

Neither is the museum or the gallery.

The paint on the wall is not what we thought.

So have courage.

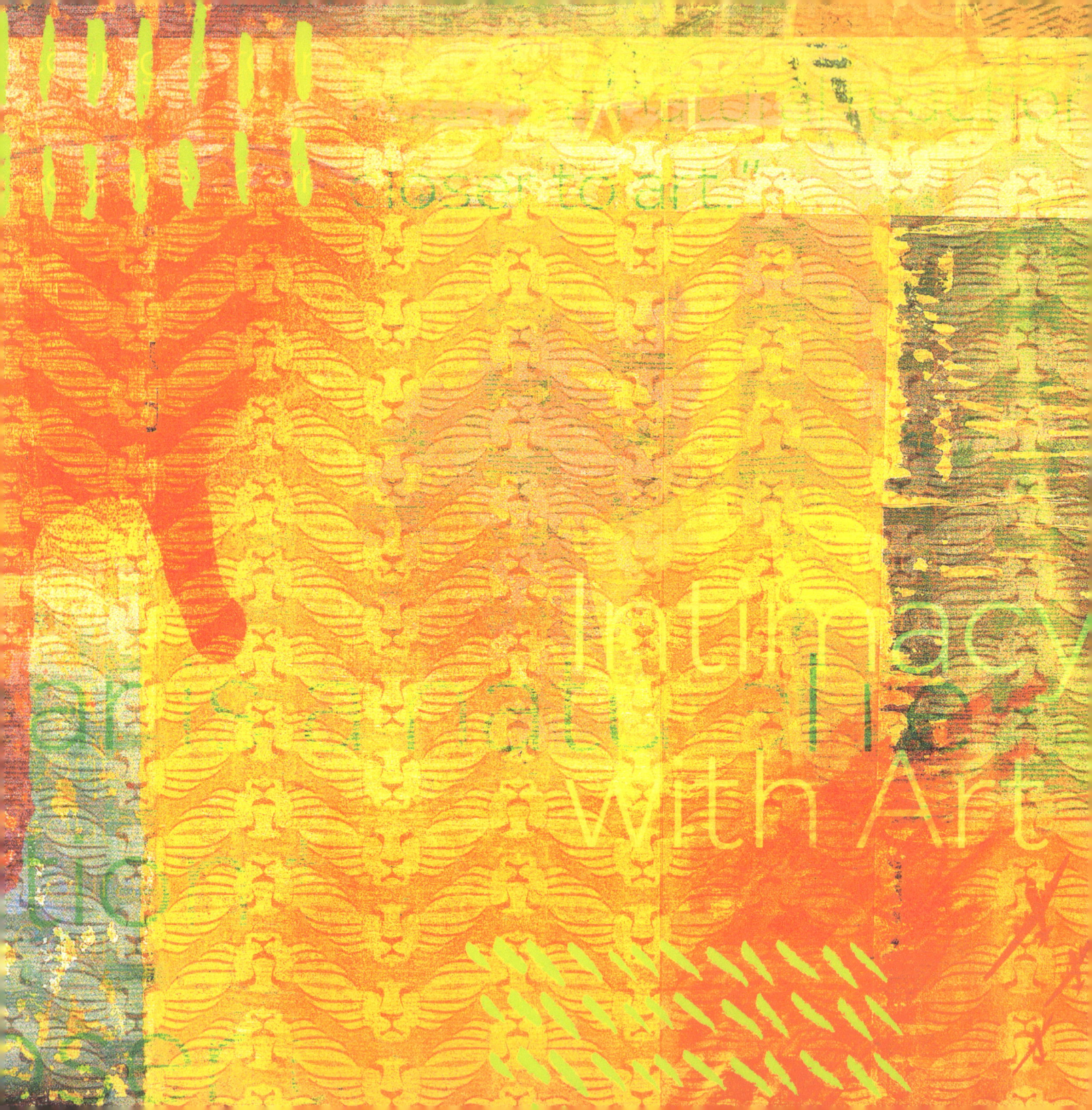

CHAPTER 4
Simple Meditations

If you find yourself feeling anxious around art, try one or more of these meditations to soothe your negative art reactions.

Say you have agreed to meet some friends for coffee and unbeknownst to you, an emerging artist has installed a small exhibition of collages throughout the cafe.

You may begin to feel nervous and start to laugh and point at the collages. You may have trouble breathing normally.

Practice with me:

This art won't hurt me—I've been through worse. This art won't hurt me—I've been through worse. This art won't hurt me—I've been through worse. This art won't hurt me—I've been through worse. This art won't hurt me—I've been through worse. This art won't hurt me—I've been through worse. This art won't hurt me—I've been through worse. This art won't hurt me—I've been through worse. This art won't hurt me—I've been through worse. This art won't hurt me—I've been through worse.

You can feel safe in the presence of art.

Let's try another one:

You have met a wonderful woman with whom you would like to pursue a relationship. She has asked you to go with her to a poetry reading being held in a large gallery.

The gallery is featuring a show of hanging sculpture made of accumulations of fabric or wire and it is visible from any seat at the reading.

You feel disoriented and you don't know what to say to her. Your mouth is dry and hands have lost their feeling.

You are afraid you are acting strangely.

Repeat to yourself:

I've survived art before, and I'll survive art this time, too.
I've survived art before, and I'll survive art this time, too.
I've survived art before, and I'll survive art this time, too.
I've survived art before, and I'll survive art this time, too.
I've survived art before, and I'll survive art this time, too.
I've survived art before, and I'll survive art this time, too.
I've survived art before, and I'll survive art this time, too.
I've survived art before, and I'll survive art this time, too.
I've survived art before, and I'll survive art this time, too.
I've survived art before, and I'll survive art this time, too.
I've survived art before, and I'll survive art this time, too.

Good.

Are you uncomfortable taking a date to a poetry reading at an art gallery?

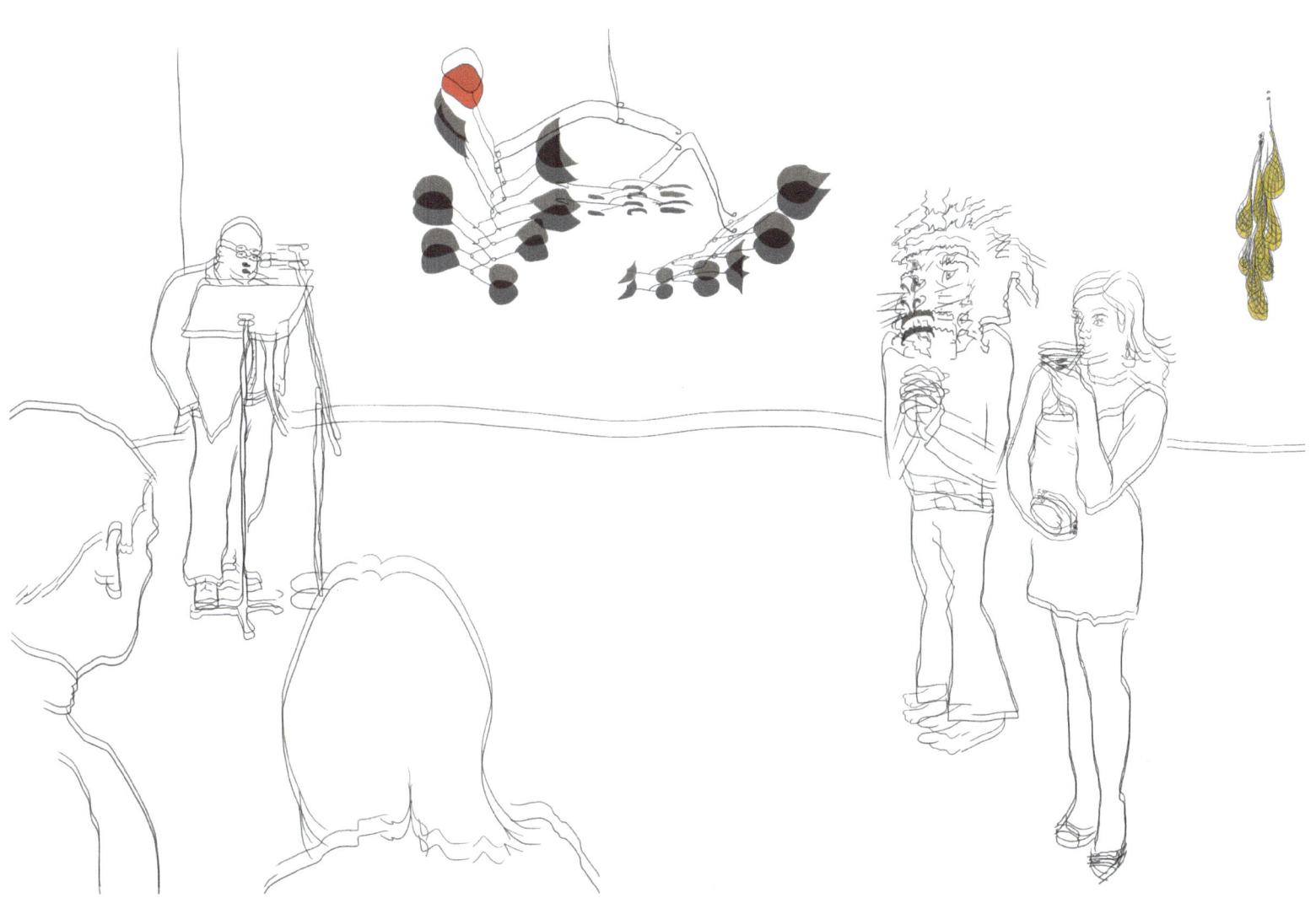

Sometimes in order to be functioning members of society, to do our jobs, or to be present at an important social gathering, we have to enter a major museum.

Occasionally you might even have to attend an event surrounded by large-scale abstract art.

You might be invited to your company's corporate headquarters in Chicago, and be required to attend a social activity including a concert at the Art Institute.

There is a reception in the museum's Contemporary Wing! You must be brave! This meditation works well in situations where you must hold yourself together against great odds.

Now for ten repetitions:

This is just art—not reality. This is just art—not reality. This is just art—not reality. This is just art—not reality. This is just art—not reality. This is just art—not reality. This is just art—not reality. This is just art—not reality. This is just art—not reality. This is just art—not reality. This is just art—not reality. This is just art—not reality.

Breathe deeply between each repetition.

Let the impact of the phrase work inside of you.

Think of the meditation as an action to release the tension you feel around the art.

Think of each breath as a unit of calmness, bringing you clarity and peace.

Keep your favorite meditation with you, written on a card. If you start to feel art anxiety, you can pull it out and repeat the meditation to yourself. You can practice at home to aid your thoughts in a new direction.

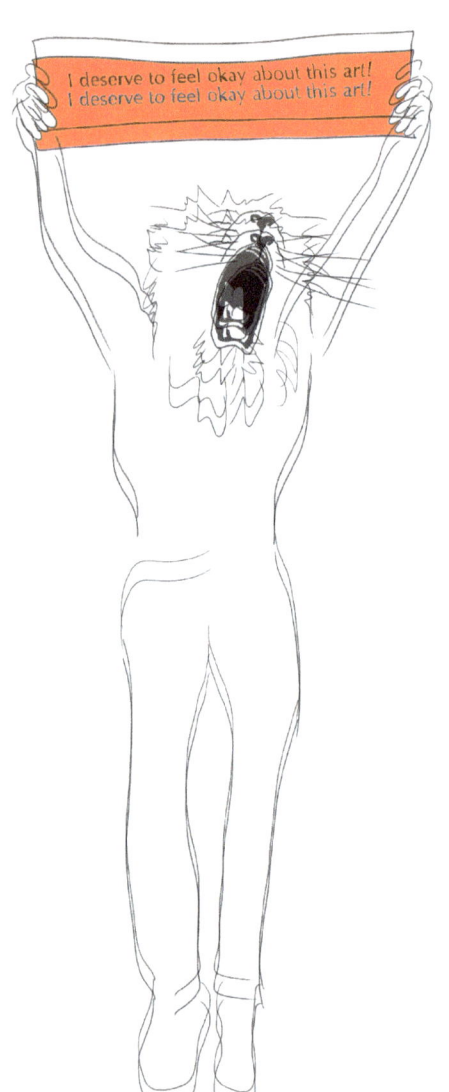

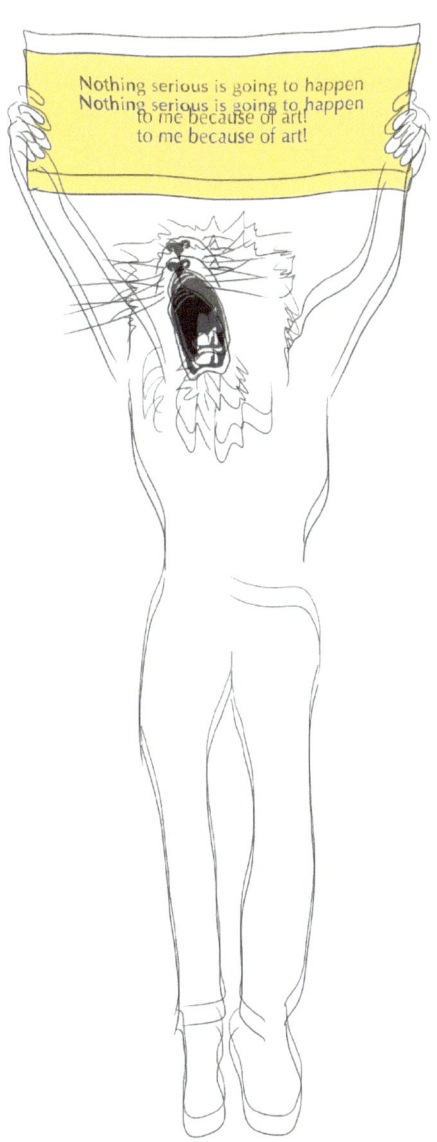

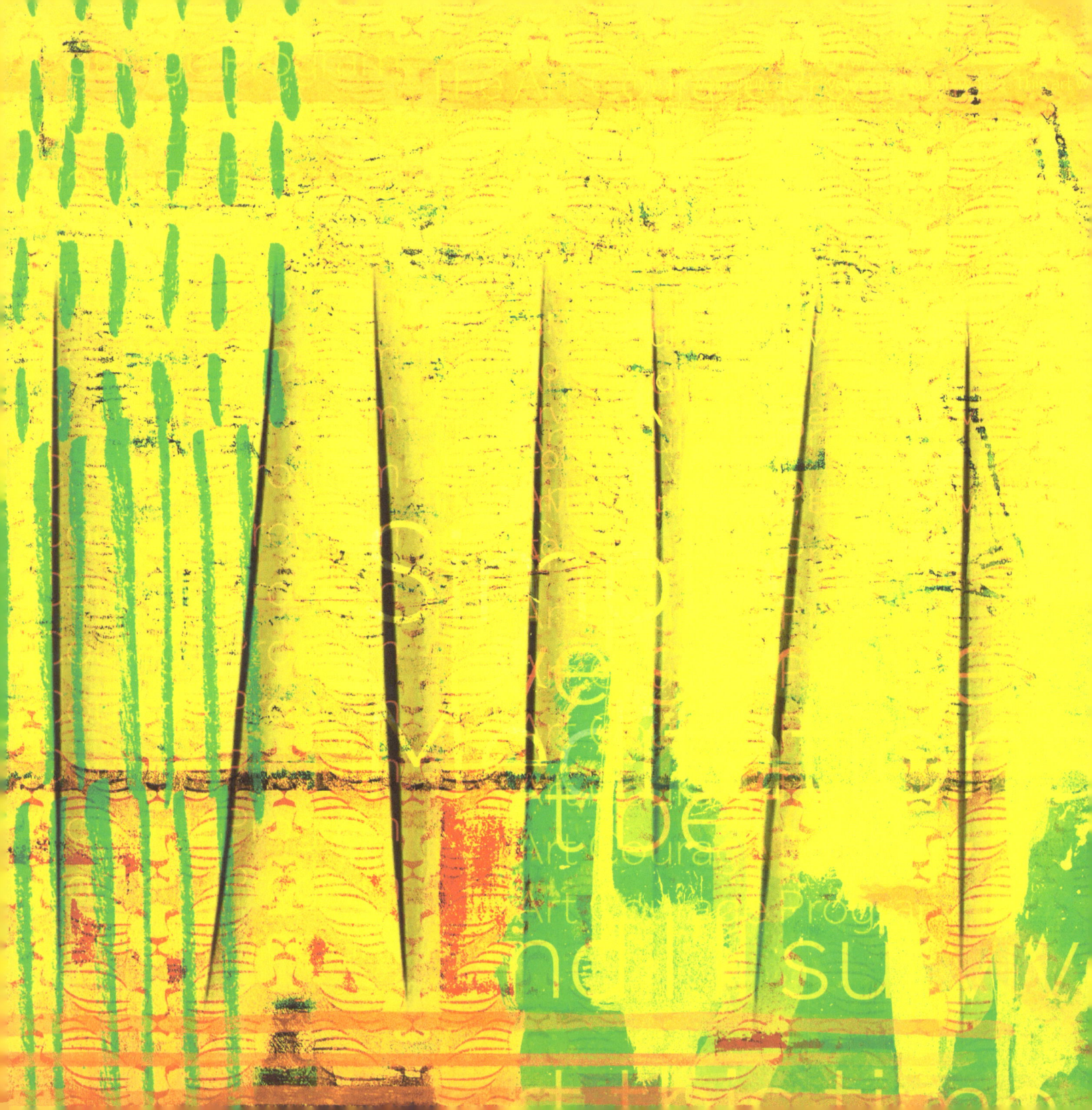

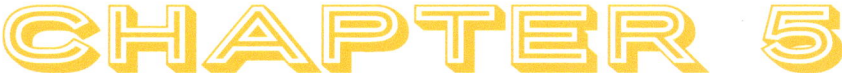
CHAPTER 5
Emergency Coping Techniques

If you are unable to arrest your art reaction before it goes beyond your personal point of no return, this is not a disaster.

You may need to excuse yourself from company and retreat to a private place while you deal with your art anxiety.

You might implement the following Emergency Coping Techniques:

a. Don't try to control or fight your symptoms—accept them and ride them out; remind yourself that art is not dangerous and your reaction will pass.

b. Call someone—express your feelings to them.

c. Move around or engage in physical activity.

d. Focus on simple objects around you or touch the floor to "ground" yourself.

e. Discharge tension by pounding your fists, crying or screaming.

f. Breathe slowly and regularly through your nose to reduce possible symptoms of hyperventilation.

g. Use positive self-talk (coping statements) in a quiet place by yourself, in conjunction with slow breathing.

h. Take an extra dose of a minor tranquilizer.

Remember, during an intense art reaction, you may feel very confused and disoriented. Try asking yourself the following questions to increase your objectivity:

Is this art I'm experiencing truly dangerous?

(Answer: No)

What is the absolute worst thing that could happen to me because of this art?

(Answer: I might have to ask for assistance in handling my reaction).

Am I telling myself anything that is making this art reaction worse?

(Answer: Probably).

What is the most supportive thing I can do for myself right now?

(Answer: Implement one of the Emergency Coping Techniques in this chapter).

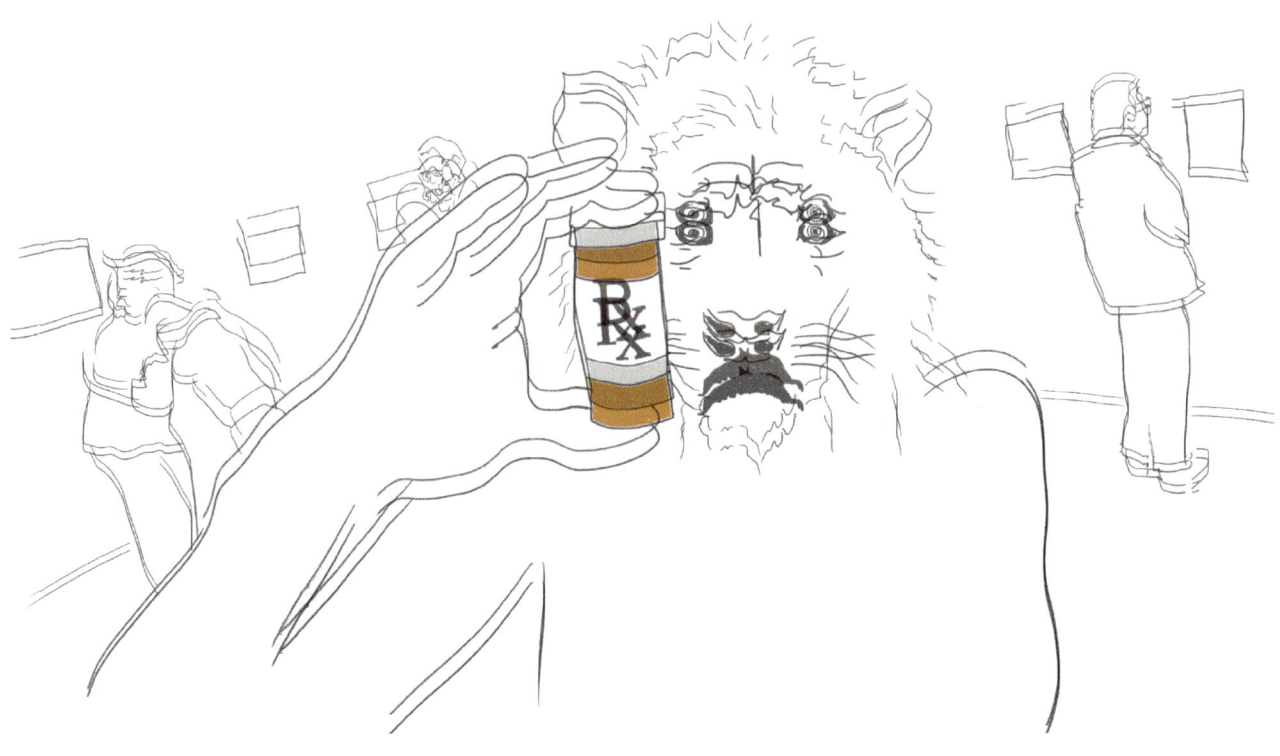

If you are unable to arrest your art reaction, try an extra dose of a minor tranquilizer.

Emergency Coping Techniques

CHAPTER 6
3-Point Plan for Alleviating Art Anxiety

If you're at a loss for what to do try this 3-Point Plan:

#1 *Accept your art reaction.*

Don't resist or fight your feelings. The more you adopt an attitude of acceptance, no matter how unpleasant the art reaction may be, the better will be your ability to cope.

Acceptance prepares you to do something proactive about your art reaction rather than get caught up in anxiety about it.

#2 *Practice deep, calm breathing.*

When art anxiety arises go right into deep, calm breathing. If you have been practicing deep, calm breathing regularly, merely initiating it provides a cue to your body to relax and disengage from a potential fight or flight response.

#3 *Use a coping strategy.*

After you begin to feel centered after abdominal breathing, use a meditation or diversion technique (for example, inhale our calming wellness fragrance* and repeat my meditations) to continue to manage your feelings.

Also, any of the Emergency Coping Strategies will reinforce the basic stance of not giving attention or energy to negative thoughts and/or uncomfortable bodily sensations.

By using coping techniques while you are in the gallery, you reinforce an attitude of mastery—instead of passive submission and victimization—in the face of the art.

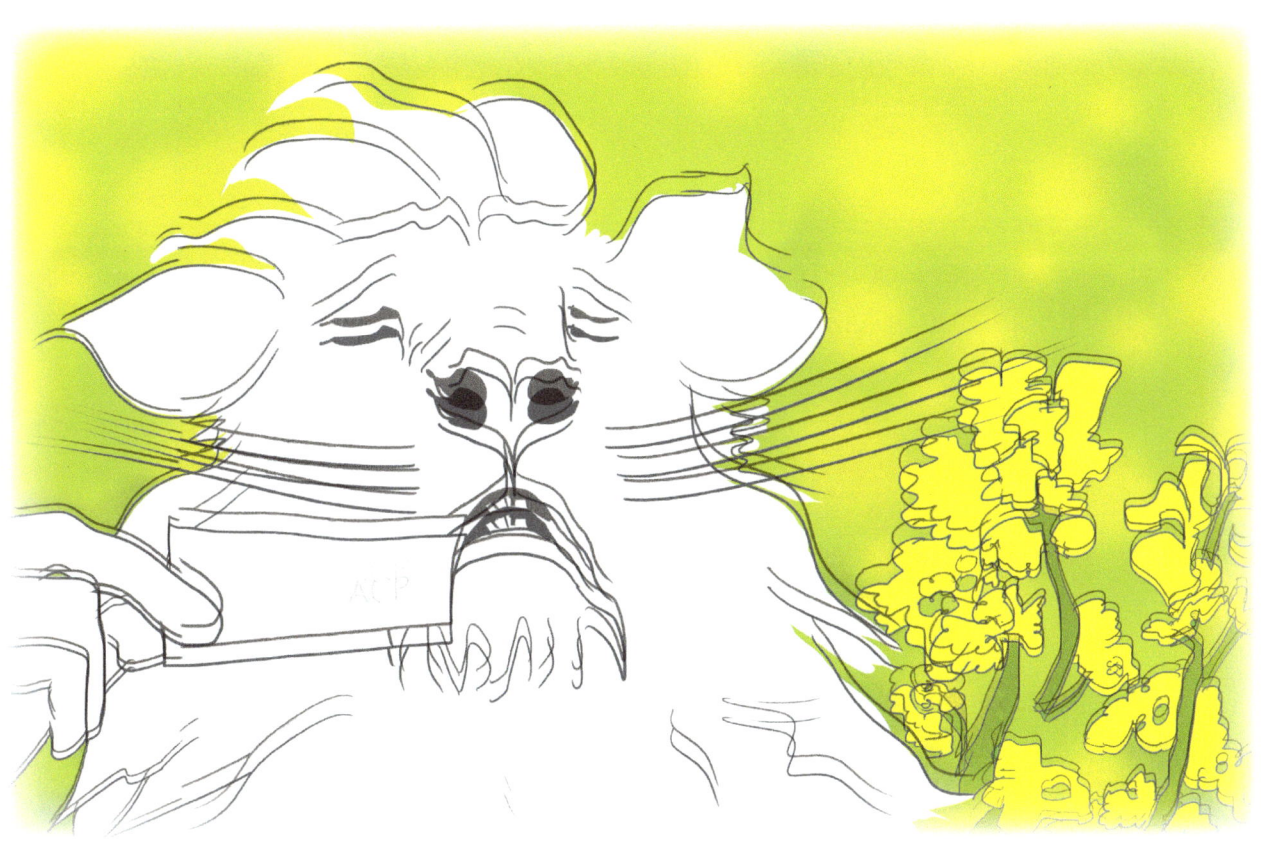

Rely on a coping strategy, such as inhaling *The Art Courage Program*'s COURAGE Series of wellness fragrances.
(See Related Products, page 67)

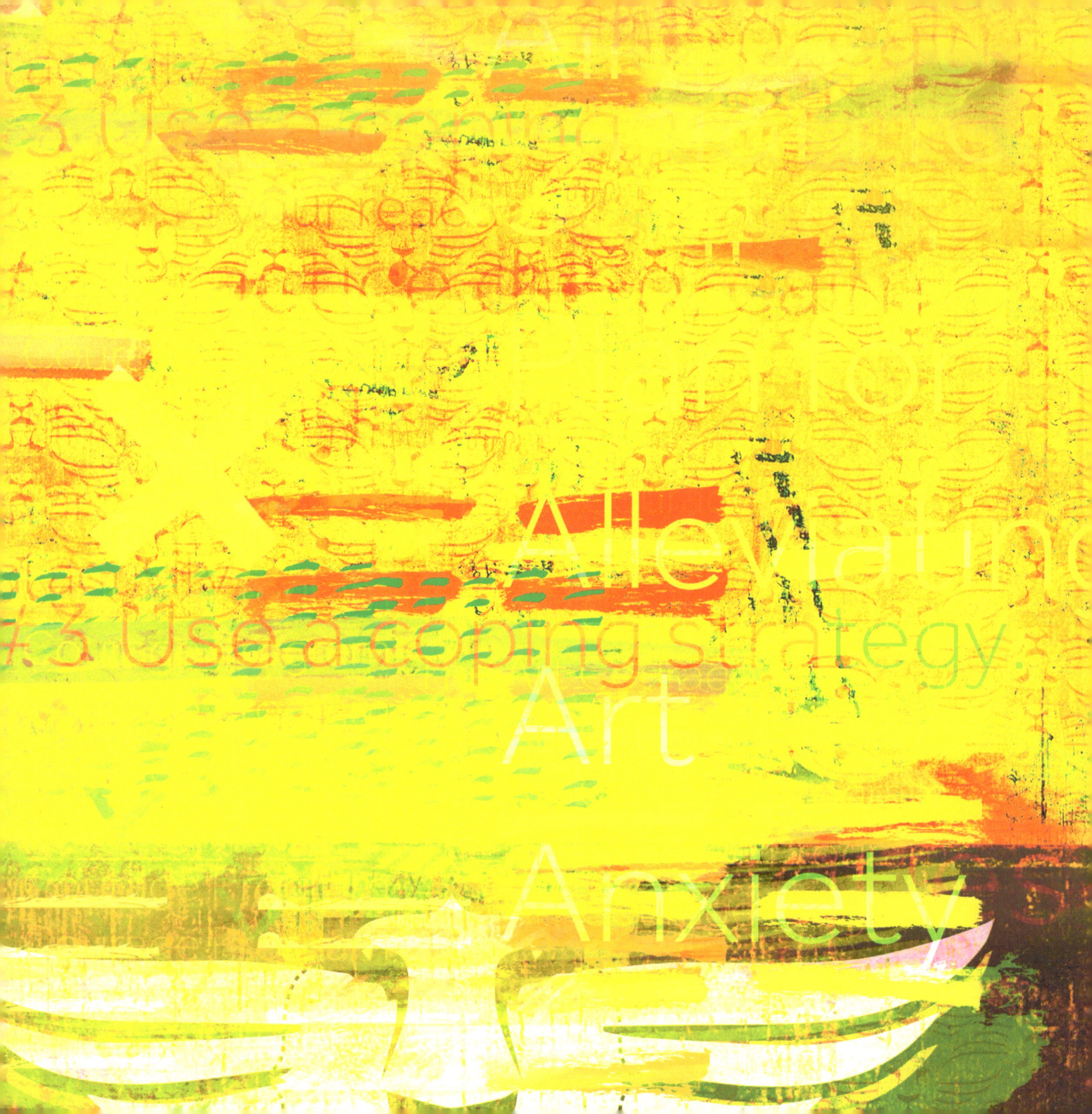

CHAPTER 7

The Art Courage Program's Dear Person Letter

Sometimes we find ourselves having to function in public or even at our workplace when we know it is likely that we may experience a negative art reaction.

I have found that it is comforting and helpful for sufferers of art reactions to carry with them a "Dear Person" letter to give to strangers or friends who may wonder why you are acting nervous or abnormal.

This is especially critical if you are afraid of art reactions interfering with your capacity to perform your job.

If you try to work without letting anyone know your problem, you may come to feel trapped in the situation—trapped by your fear of what other people might think if you "lost it."

A "Dear Person" letter can lift the burden off of you having to put the words together to explain yourself when you may be experiencing a great deal of discomfort.

On the following page is a model on which to base your own "Dear Person" letter.

You can leave the name blank or fill in whatever you need (your boss, a group leader, someone at church):

Dear [   ]:

I want to tell you something about myself. I have a problem with my negative reaction to art. This is not a mental illness, but a kind of anxiety that manifests physical and psychological symptoms:

Although 5 in 100 people suffer from this reaction, some people have not heard of the condition. It is difficult for me to talk about it, especially if I am feeling bad, but sharing this information is important to me.

A Negative Art Reaction is similar to claustrophobia, except that my reactions can be triggered by many things, such as paintings, poetry, large sculpture, gallery spaces, graffiti and/or many other unexpected things. I can neither anticipate nor control these reactions. Because these reactions are extremely uncomfortable, sometimes terrifying and always embarrassing, I have begun avoiding situations that might arouse them.

I have found help for this problem and am making progress. At this point I am doing some things and want to do even more, but I still need a way out of art situations that are frightening to me. I have found that when other people understand that I may need to leave an uncomfortable art situation, I can do better and it helps with my recovery.

It is extremely important to me to feel free to leave any given art situation at any time, no matter how innocuous the situation may appear. I don't ask you to understand my condition, but I would appreciate your help.

In telling you this, I am not soliciting your sympathy, but I would like your moral support as I work toward recovery. I realize that the way I confront art may seem confusing and even inappropriate to you. Be assured that I have found *The Art Courage Program* I am using now is helping me to recover. With your acceptance, you will be working with me in conquering this problem.

Sincerely,

[Your Name]

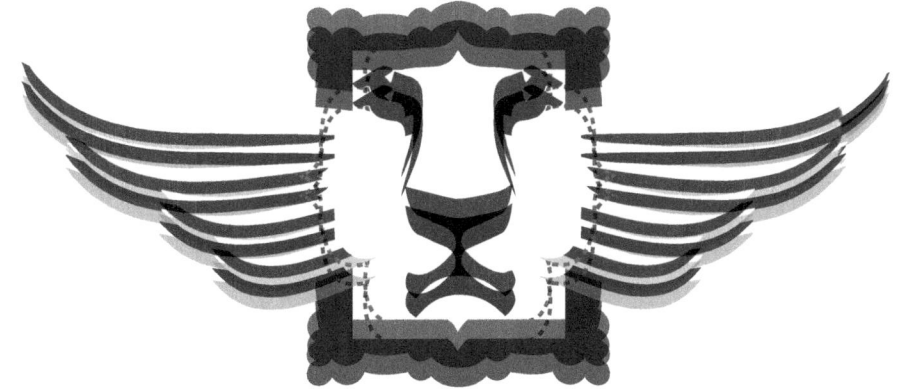

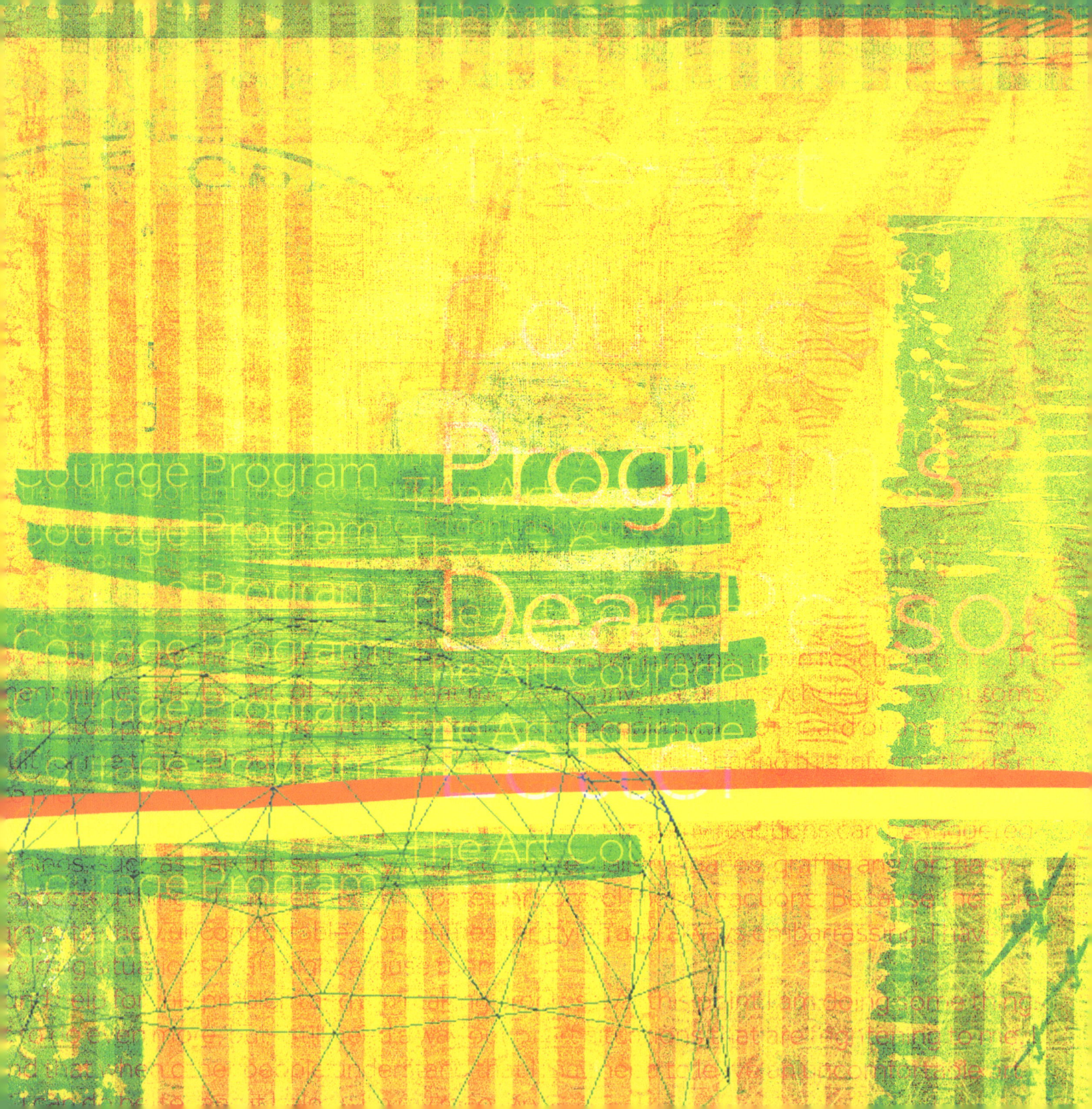

CHAPTER 8
The Art Courage Program's Write Your Own Prescription

At the end of any workshop with sufferers of Art Anxiety, I write out a prescription.

It includes a list of sensory supplements, instructions about diet and food preparation, and advice on meditation and exercise.

Among my recommendations there are always action/release techniques, approaches and attitudes that each person has told me—which she *already knows* are helpful. These are the ones I am asking you to record here now, at the end of this program.

I suggest you take some time now to write out your own prescription.

First listen to the instructions and follow my verbal example.

Next, sit quietly and close your eyes.

Breathe deeply and slowly for three to four minutes. Remember, each breath is a unit of calm.

Let's begin.

Put your name at the top of a piece of paper, just as a physician would on a prescription pad, and write: "What Already Makes Me Feel Happy and Whole Around Art."

Now begin listing in short sentences activities you already do that are helpful to you, modifying them to make them fit into the needs you now feel in connection to art.

Add activities like meditation for action/release or deep, calm breathing which may have appealed to you as read this book.

And just as on a prescription pad, write down the frequency and duration of the activity that you're proposing.

Be realistic, and be a bit brave too.

How high was your score on your Personal Audit for Self-Liberation? If you *feel* it was high, you may want choose six to eight wellness activities to perform on a daily basis, to aid you in your healing and ongoing well-being.

You might write on your prescription to do yoga every day before you walk past the sculpture in front of your building.

You might write that you will go to Quaker meeting every week, and to bring your Dear Person letter with you for the meeting leader.

You might practice deep, calm breath unit techniques two or three times a day or whenever you have a negative reaction.

At the end, sign your prescription. If you'd like, copy your prescription and put it on your refrigerator or desk.

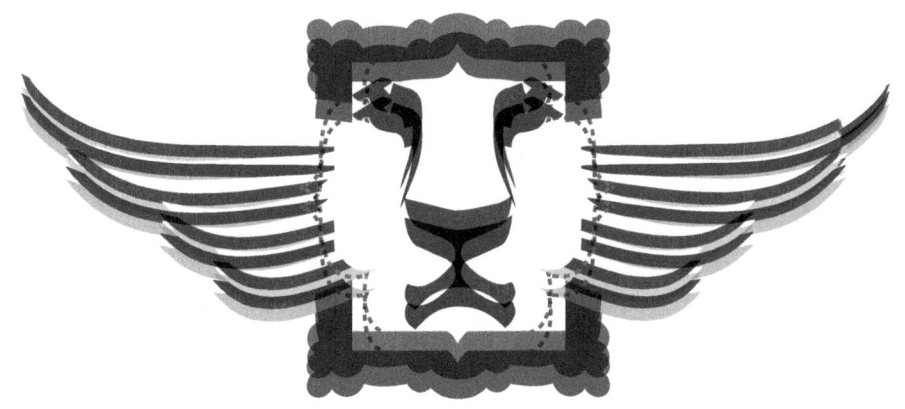

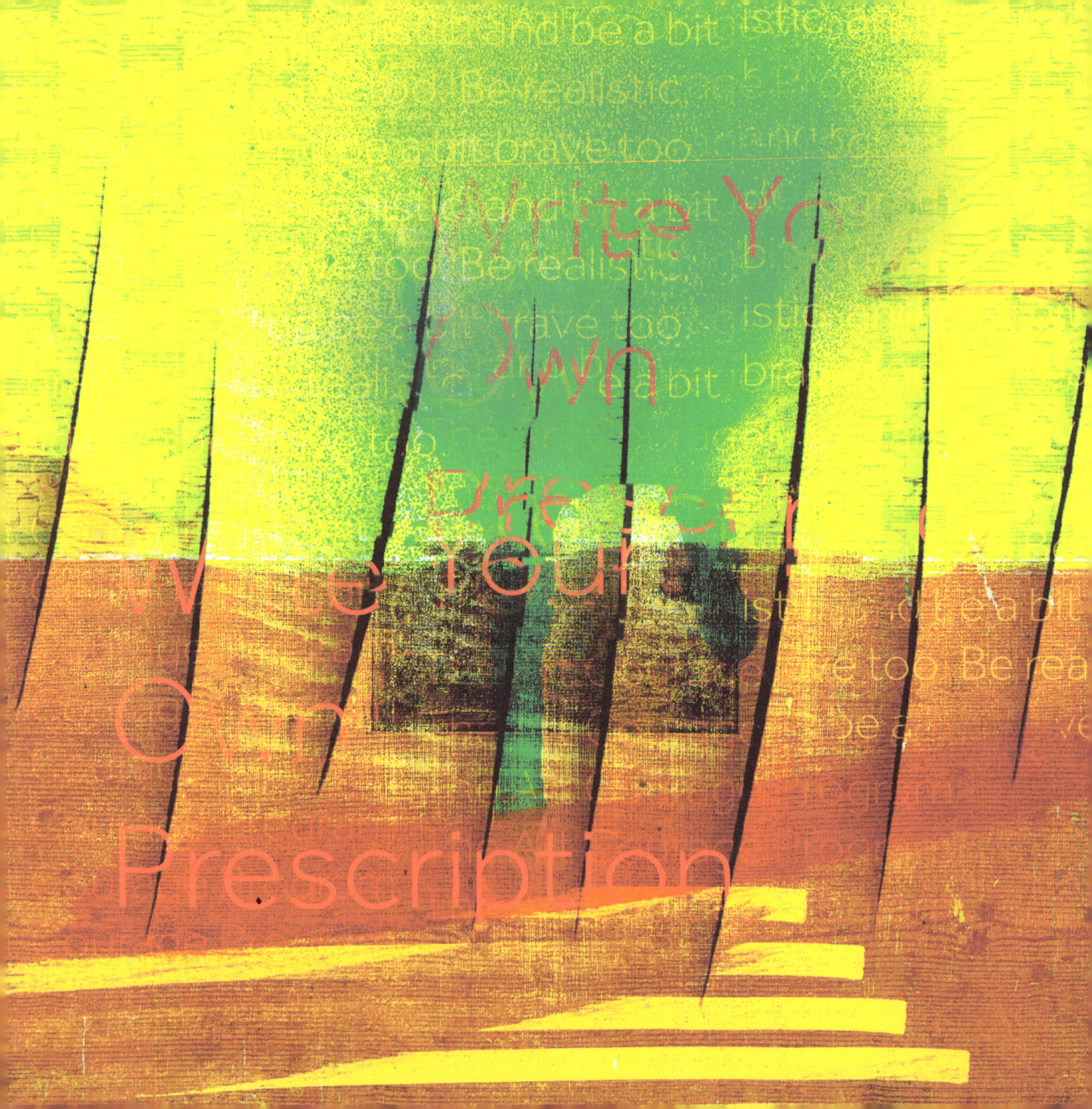

CONCLUSION

We all want to live in a world wherein we do not just exist, but we celebrate existence.

If art anxiety is preventing you from experiencing real pleasure in life, then dedicate yourself to *The Art Courage Program*.

Make it your practice.

Remember, in the paradigm of heightened awareness the only thing that has beginning or end is perception itself. Attaining heightened levels of awareness is a goal that can be facilitated through a comprehensive set of wellness modalities.

c *(pronounced /k/)* offers a proprietary line of aural, olfactory, visual, and physical modalities that promises a path to well-being.

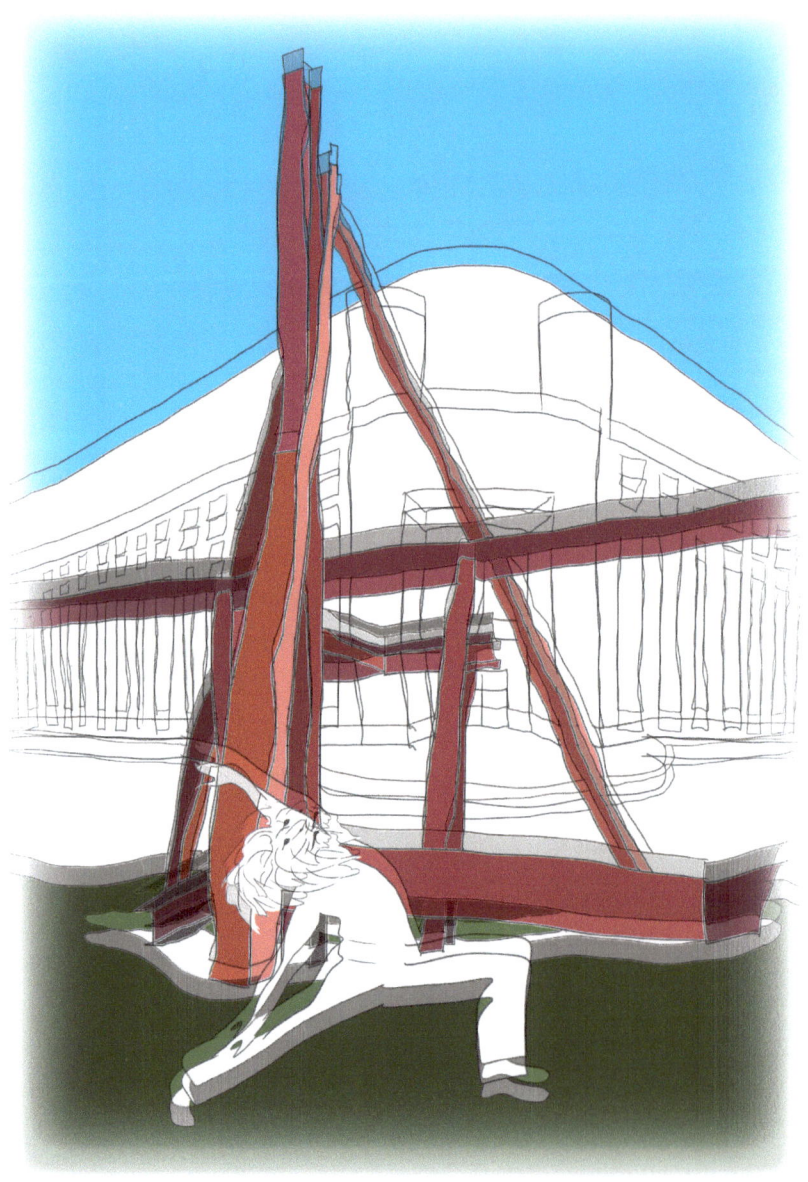

Practice yoga before you walk past that public artwork.
Practice yoga before you walk past that public artwork.

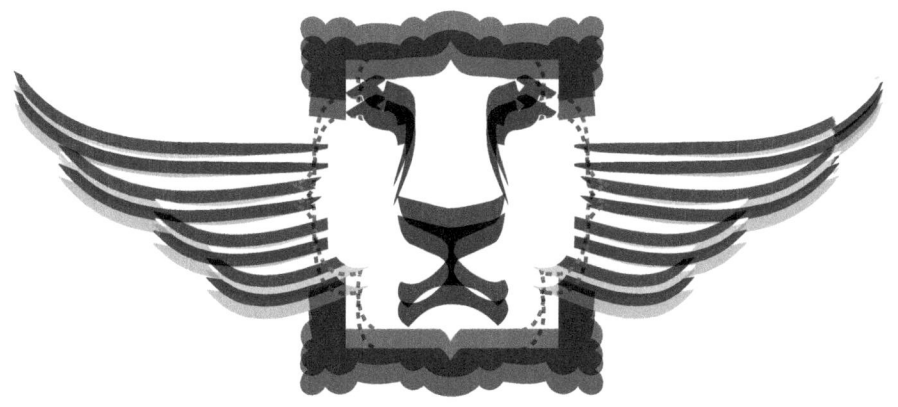

We all want to
live in a world
wherein we
not just exist
but we exist

Make it your practice
Make it your practice
Make it your
Make it your

AUTHOR BIOGRAPHIES

Katharine Whitcomb is an Emotional Language Therapist (ELT), whose therapeutic manifestos include *Saints of South Dakota & Other Poems* (Bluestem Press, 2001), *Hosannas* (Parallel Press, 1999) and *Lamp of Letters* (Floating Bridge Press, 2009). She is the co-facilitator of *A Sense of Place: The Washington State Geospatial Poetry Anthology*, and the senior prescription writer at *Cascadia Chronicle: A Geospatial Journal of Place, Environment and Imagination*. She has had research published in many journals including *The Paris Review* and in anthologies, including *Fire On Her Tongue*. She expresses regret that she is no longer able to take on new patients.

Brian Goeltzenleuchter founded *Contraposto Living* in 1998. The company's mission is to enhance personal and institutional equilibrium through a proprietary line of products, services and educational tools. The retail wing of *Contraposto Living* is dedicated to refashioning the greatest achievements of world culture into consumable home accents through an ever-growing line of candles, soap, fragrances, and garden sculpture. The company's institutional wing has received international acclaim for its proprietary line of services and educational tools designed explicitly for cultural institutions and the people they employ. More information can be found at www.contrapostoliving.com.

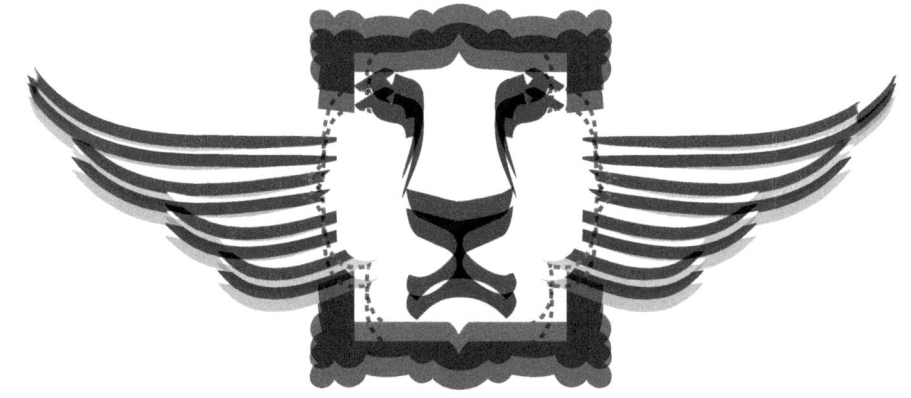

RELATED PRODUCTS

Additional modalities from c *(pronounced /k/)* line of wellness products:

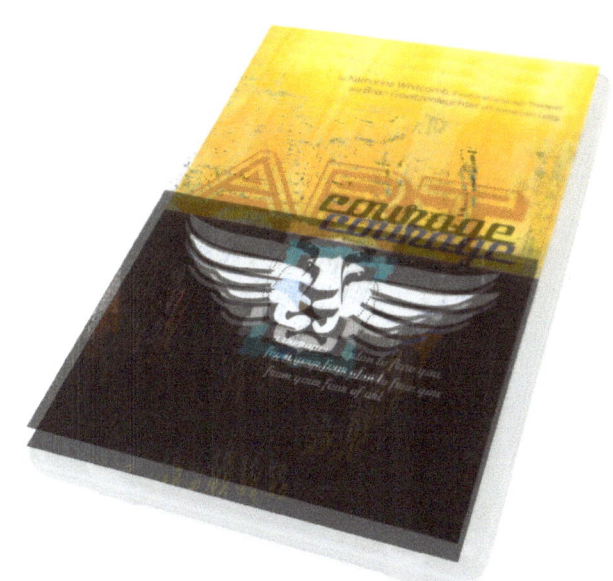

The Art Courage Program Audio Cassette with MP3

The Art Courage Program is available as a special edition audio cassette with MP3 download card. This recording features the text of the program read by co-author Katharine Whitcomb. A perfect accompaniment to the book—this recording can come with you on your iPod or in your car. A useful tool for therapeutic meditation.

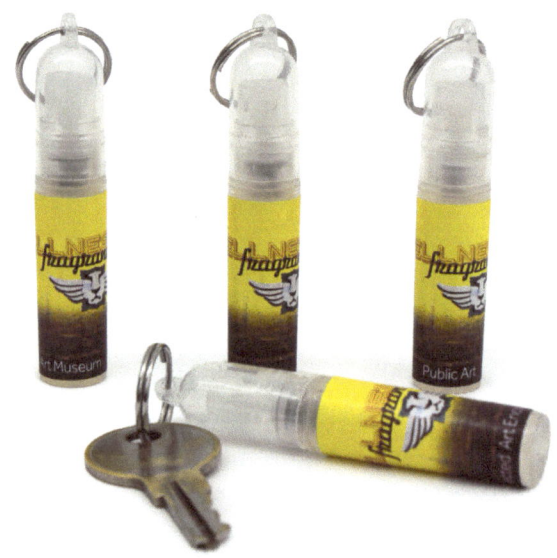

The COURAGE Series of Travel-Sized Wellness Fragrances

Inhale one of c *(pronounced /k/)*'s Wellness Fragrances designed explicitly for users of *The Art Courage Program*. The series contains the following four therapeutic fragrances: *ART EVENT, ART MUSEUM, PUBLIC ART*, and *UNEXPECTED ART ENCOUNTER*. By exploiting the precognitive sense of smell, this travel-sized fragrance can be applied at regular intervals to cleanse the environmental ambiance or used as a focal point in your meditation practice.

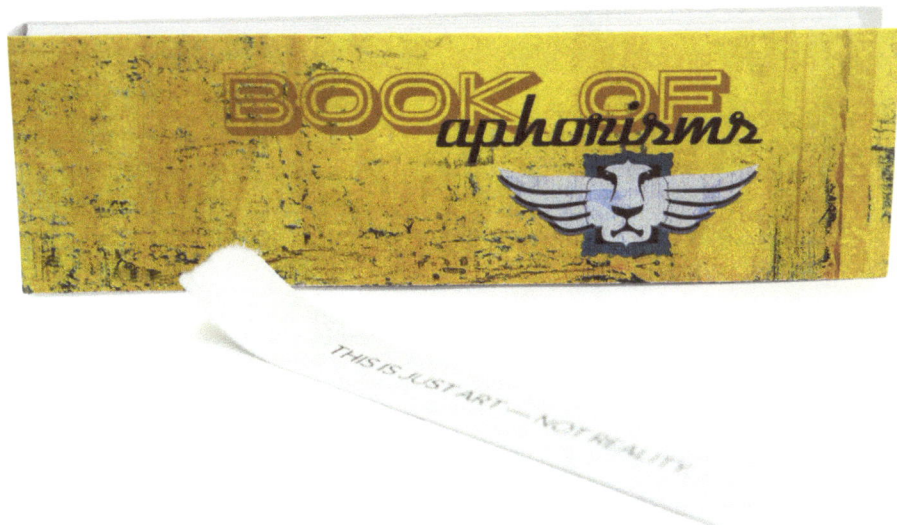

The Art Courage Program's Book of Aphorisms

Don't be caught in an art emergency without your ACP tools! This portable tear-out book is designed to be used with the COURAGE Series of Wellness Fragrances. The ACP aphorisms are printed on perfume blotter paper in a handy booklet, and can be sprayed with any one of the four therapeutic fragrances. Essential remedies on the go for whatever art anxiety you are experiencing!

70

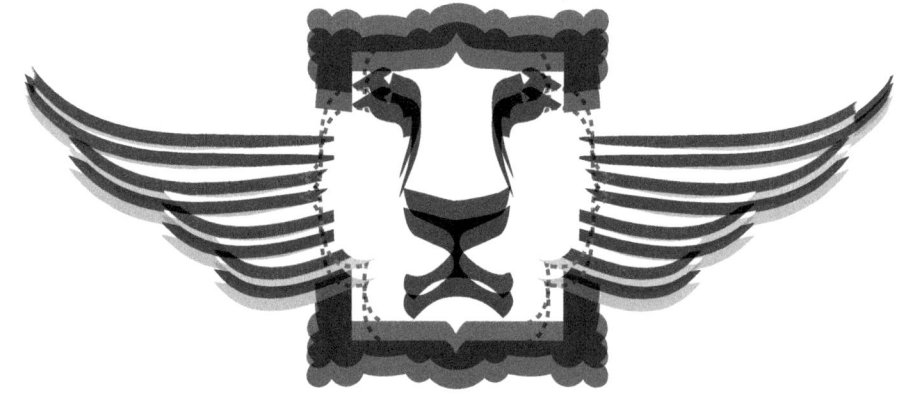

www.ingramcontent.com/pod-product-compliance
Lightning Source LLC
Chambersburg PA
CBHW051917210526
45473CB00006B/2049